CROCHET DOG SWEATERS

Linda Memmel

AuthorHouse™
1663 Liberty Drive
Bloomington, IN 47403
www.authorhouse.com
Phone: 1-800-839-8640

©2011 Linda Memmel. All rights reserved.

No part of this book may be reproduced, stored in a retrieval system, or transmitted by any means without the written permission of the author.

First published by AuthorHouse   2/22/2011

ISBN: 978-1-4520-2097-6 (sc)

Printed in the United States of America
Bloomington, Indiana

This book is printed on acid-free paper.

Crochet Dog Sweaters

Published by AuthorHouse
First paperback edition

Distributed

The written instructions, photographs, designs, patterns, and projects in this volume are intended for the personal use of the reader and may be reproduced for the purpose only. Any other use, especially, commercial use is forbidden under law without permission of copyright holder.

Every effort has been made to ensure that all the information in this book is accurate. However due to differing conditions, tools, and individual stills, the publisher cannot be responsible for any injuries, losses, and other damages that may result from the use of the information in this book.

If you have questions or comments about this book, please contact the publisher Authorhouse.

Crochet Dog Sweaters

By Linda Memmel

DEDICATION

This work is dedicated to my mother, Lorraine Mundt, and Grandmother Rose, who passed on a love of crocheting.

I am grateful to my husband, Larry, two daughters, Lisa and Leslie, and to the memory of Bentley and Tucker. Without their patience, understanding, support and most of all love, the completion of this work would not have been possible.

Contents

Dedication	2
Foreword	4
Introduction	5
Basic Stitches Instructions	6
Helpful Subjection	7
Red and Black Valentine Dog Sweater	9
Bright Green Shamrock Dog Sweater	19
4th Of July Sweater	27
Snowman Christmas Dog Sweater	35

Foreword

Introduction

Taking the time and making a special homemade gift for someone special is always rewarding, and takes on special significance and value.

So, begin right now, and crochet a tender loving sweater for your very favorite dog. The wearable projects will keep your loveable dog warm and cozy throughout the cold winter months.

Basic Stitches Instructions

CHAIN STICH (ch)

Step1: From the picture shown yarn over hook and draw the yarn through to form (ch made) makes a new loop.
Repeat the (ch) as required, but do not count the slip knot as a (ch).
SINGLE CROCHET (sc)

STEP 1: From the picture shown insert hook at the 2nd chain from hook at the 2nd chain from hook to make the first sc.

STEP 2: Then draw yarn through stitch.

STEP 3: Draw through 2 loops on hook, and repeat to make a new (sc).

DOUBLE CROCHET (dc)

From the picture shown, yart over hook on the 4th chain from hook. Yarn through the 3 loops on hook. Yarn over hook and draw through 2 loops, yarn over through last 2 loops, (dc) made. Repeat to make a new (dc)

Helpful Subjection

Buying Yarn
When purchasing yarn buy extra amount in the same dye lot.

Joining Yarn
When you are crocheting and you need to add a new color, work a stitch up to the last step, pickup the new yarn and complete the last step of the stitch. Keep both loose ends on the wrong side to be woven into the piece later.

Washing Instructions
Hand washing and Drying
Turn garment inside out wash gently in cold water, using a mild detergent. Rinse in cold water, squeeze and spread garment flat on a smooth surface, allow it to dry thoroughly.

Crochet Hook Sizes

Continental	U.S.
2.25mm	B-1
2.75mm	C-2
3.25mm	D-3
3.5mm	E-4
4mm	F-5
4.5mm	G-6
5mm	7
5.5mm	I-9
6mm	J-10
6.5mm	K-10 ½
8mm	L-11
9mm	M/N-13
10mm	N/P-15
15mm	P/Q
16mm	Q
19mm	S

Letter or number may vary by manufacturer.
For accurate and consistent sizing, rely on the Millimeter (mm) size.

RED AND BLACK VALENTINE DOG SWEATER

RED AND BLACK VALENTINE DOG SWEATER

Your crochet talent brings a lasting warmth to your dog with a dog weather made with love, and of course. Easy care yarn that will also rekindling visions of valentine day.

FINISHED SIZE
Approximately length small 20 x 21

Note: Length is measured from the base of neck of the dog to base of the dogs tail.

Size H Crochet Hook

Hot RED Medium

Note Heart: To change color work you of last st in prev color with new color, dropping prev color to back of work. Carry BLACK color loosely across the row.

ADDREVIATIONS
dc   double crochet
sc   single crochet
ch   chain (s)
sl st   slip stitch
dec   decrease (s)

12

DIRECTIONS

Begin ch 37 loosely with color RED yarn about 11" long.
Foundation Row:
With RED yarn sc in the 2nd ch from the hook and in each ch sc across ch 2 turn.

ROW 1: With BLACK yarn 2 dc in the 3rd ch from hook in the back ch, and in each ch back dc across, last ch 2 in the back ch, ch 2 turn.

ROW 2: With BLACK yarn, 2 dc in the 3rd ch, dc across, last ch 2 dc, ch 2 turn.

ROW 3: With BLACK yarn, 2 dc in the 3rd ch, dc across, last ch 2 dc, ch 2 turn.

ROW 4: With BLACK yarn, 2 dc in the 3rd ch, dc across, last ch 2 dc, ch 2 turn. Make it 22" long.

ROW 5: With BLACK yarn 2 dc in the 3rd ch, dc across, last ch 2 dc, ch 2 turn.

ROW 6: With BLACK yarn 2 dc in the 3rd ch dc across, last ch 2 dc, ch 2 turn.

ROW 7: With BLACK yarn 2 dc in the 3rd ch dc across, last ch 2 dc, ch 2 turn.

ROW 8: With BLACK yarn 2 dc in the 3rd ch dc across, last ch 2 dc, ch 2 turn.

ROW 9: With BLACK yarn 2 dc in the 3rd ch, dc across, last ch 2 dc, ch 2 turn.

ROW 10: With BLACK yarn 2 dc in the 3rd ch, dc across, last ch 2 dc, ch 2 turn.

ROW 11: With BLACK yarn 2 dc in the 3rd ch, dc across,
Last ch 2dc, ch 2 turn.

ROW 12: With BLACK yarn 2 dc in the 3rd ch, dc across, last ch 2 dc, ch 2 turn.

RED HEART:

ROW 13: With BLACK yarn ac across 28 ch, and on 29 dc in RED, 30 ch dc in BLACK, to the end ch 2 turn.

ROW 14: With BLACK yarn dc across 27 ch, and on 28, 29, 30, dc in RED, 31 ch dc in BLACK to the end, ch 2 turn.

ROW 15: With BLACK yarn dc across 25 ch, and on 26, 27, 28, 29, 30, 31, 32, in RED, 33 ch dc in BLACK to the end, ch 2 turn.

ROW 16: With BLACK yarn dc across 23 ch, and on 24, 25, 26, 27, 28, 29, 30, 31, 32, 33, 34, in RED, 35 ch dc in BLACK to the end, ch 2 turn.

ROW 17: With BLACK yarn dc across 21 ch, and on 22, 23, 24, 25, 26, 27, 28, 29, 30, 31, 32, 33, 34, 35, 36 in RED, 37 ch dc in BLACK to the end, ch 2 turn.

ROW 18: With BLACK yarn dc across 21 ch, and on 22, 23, 24, 25, 26, 27, 28, 29, 30, 31, 32, 33, 34, 35, 36 in RED, 37 ch dc in BLACK to the end, ch 2 turn.

ROW 19: With BLACK yarn dc across 21 ch, and on
22, 23, 24, 25, 26, 27, 28 in RED, 29 ch in BLACK dc 30, 31, 32, 33, 34, 35, 36 in RED 37 ch dc in BLACK to the end, ch 2 turn.

ROW 20: With BLACK yarn dc across 23 ch, and on 24, 25, 26, 27 in RED 28, 29, 30 ch in BLACK dc 31, 32, 33, 34 in RED 35 ch dc in BLACK to the end, ch 2 turn.

ROW 21: With BLACK yarn dc in the 3rd ch, dc across to the end, ch 2 turn.

ROW 22: With BLACK yarn dc in the 3rd ch dc, across to the end ch 2 turn.

ROW 23: With BLACK yarn dc in the 3rd ch dc, across to the end to the end.

RIGHT SIDE OF THE SHOULDER LEG CUFFS

ROW 24: With BLACK yarn 3rd ch, dc 3 across, ch 2 turn.

ROW 25: With BLACK yarn 3rd ch, dc 3 across, ch 2 turn.

ROW 26: With BLACK yarn 3rd ch, dc 3 across, ch 2 turn.

ROW 27: With BLACK yarn 3rd ch, dc 3 across, ch 2 turn.

ROW 28: With BLACK yarn 3rd ch, dc 3 across, ch 2 turn.

ROW 29: With BLACK yarn 3rd ch, dc 3 across, ch 2 turn.

MIDDLE

ROW 24: With BLACK yarn skip ch 1-13, on the 14 ch, dc in the next 24 chs, ch 2 turn.

ROW 25: With BLACK yarn skip ch 1-13, on the 14 ch, dc in the next 24 chs, ch 2 turn.

ROW 26: With BLACK yarn skip ch 1-13, on the 14 ch, dc in the next 24 chs, ch 2 turn.

Row 27: With BLACK yarn skip ch 1-13, on the 14 ch dc in the next 24 chs, ch 2 turn.

ROW 28: With BLACK yarn skip ch 1-13, on the 14 ch dc in the next 24 chs, ch 2 turn.

ROW 29: With BLACK yarn skip ch 1-13, on the 14 ch dc in the next 24 chs, ch 2 turn.

LEFT SIDE OF THE SHOULD LEG CUFFS

ROW 24: With BLACK yarn 3rd ch, dc across to the end, ch 2 turn.

ROW 25: With BLACK yarn 3rd ch, dc across to the end, ch 2 turn.

ROW 26: With BLACK yarn 3rd ch, dc across to the end, ch 2 turn.

ROW 27: With BLACK yarn 3rd ch, dc across to the end, ch 2 turn.

ROW 28: With BLACK yarn 3rd ch, dc across to the end, ch 2 turn.

ROW 29: With BLACK yarn 3rd ch, dc across to the end, ch 2 turn.

RIGHT LEG

ROW 1: With RED yarn ch 28, in the 3rd ch dc, across to the end, ch 2 turn.

ROW 2: With BLACK yarn, in the 3rd ch dc, across to the end, ch 2 turn.

ROW 3: With BLACK yarn, in the 3rd ch dc, across to the end, ch 2 turn.

ROW 4: With BLACK yarn, in the 3rd ch dc, across to the end, ch 2 turn.

ROW 5: With BLACK yarn, in the 3rd ch dc, across to the end, ch 2 turn.

ROW 6: With BLACK yarn, in the 3rd ch dc, across to the end, ch 2 turn.

ROW 7: With BLACK yarn, in the 3rd ch dc, across to the end, ch 2 turn.

ROW 8: With BLACK yarn, in the 3rd ch dc, across to the end, ch 2 turn.
LEFT LEG

ROW 1: With RED yarn ch 28, in the 3rd ch, dc, across to the end, ch 2 turn.

ROW 2: With BLACK yarn, in the 3rd ch dc, across to the end, ch 2 turn.

ROW 3-8: Repeat Row 2.

ASSEMBLY RIGHT LEG

The same as the right leg.

NECK

ROW 30: Tie on the BLACK yarn, ch 2 in the 3rd ch dc. Also, dc around the side of the leg (making the right and left legs holes) dc to the end, ch 2 turn.

ROW 31: With BLACK yarn, dc in the 3rd ch, dc around to the end, ch 2 turn.

ROW 32: With BLACK yarn, dc in the 3rd ch, dc around to the end, ch 2 turn.

ROW 33: With BLACK yarn, dc in the 3rd ch, dc around to the end, ch 2 turn.

ROW 34: With BLACK yarn, dc to the end, skip the 2 chs dc in the last ch, ch 2 turn.

ROW 35: With RED yarn, dc to the end, skip the 2 chs, dc in the last ch, ch 2 turn.

ROW 36: With RED yarn, dc in the back hook in the end, ch 2 turn.

ROW 37: With BLACK yarn, dc in the end, skip the 2 chs, dc in the last ch, ch 2 turn.

ROW 38: With BLACK yarn, dc in the back hook to the end, ch 2 turn.

ROW 39: With RED yarn dc in the end, skip the 2 chs, dc in the last ch, ch 2 turn.

ROW 40: With RED yarn dc in the back hook to the end, ch 2 turn.

NECK RUFFLE

At row 30 RED yarn, right side pick-up ch. Sc, dc, sc, in the 1 ch, skip a ch and again sc, dc, sc, in the 1 ch* repeat in the end.

FINISHING

At this time try on the sweater on the dog, and see how it looks and fits. With the sweater body put the right sides together start at Row 12 to Row 33 sl st together with BLACK yarn.

ENJOY!!!!!

BRIGHT GREEN SHAMROCK DOG SWEATER

WITH THE LUCK OF THE IRISH WOULD HAVE IT, KEEP YOUR DOG WARM IN THE MARCH WIND.

BRIGHT GREEN SHAMROCK DOG SWEATER

FINISHED SIZE
Approximately length small 20 x 21

Note Length is measured from the base of neck of the dog to base of the dogs tail.

MATERIALS
2 Emerald Green Yarn
1 White Yarn

Size G Crochet Hook
1 Steel Crochet Hook Size 00

ADDREVIATIONS
ch   chains (s)
yo   yarn over
sc   single crochet
lp   loop (s)
sl st   slip stitch

Shamrock Dog Sweater

X in WHITE

BRIGHT GREEN SHAMROCK DOG SWEATER

DIRECTIONS

AFGHAN STITCH FOR THE SHAMROCKS
With GREEN yarn ch 43 loosely.

ROW 1 Step 1: Keeping all lps on hook, pull up alp through top lp only, in 2nd ch from hook and each ch across same number of lps and ch. Do not turn.

STEP 2: Yo and pull through first lp on hook, *yo and pull through 2 lps on hook, rep from * across (1lp rem on hook for first lp of next row). Do no turn.

ROW 2: Step 1: Keeping all lps on hook, pull up a lp from under 2nd vertical bar,* pull up a lp from under next vertical bar, rep from * across. Do not turn.

STEP 2: Rep Step 2 of Row 1. Rep both steps of Row 2 for required for 11 Rows. Fasten off after last row by working a sl st in each bar across. When the 11 Rows are finished, it is a perfect grid for cross-stitch for the 3 WHTIE shamrocks.

EMBROIDERY STITCHES
To embellish a crocheted piece with embroidery, thread a large-eyed yarn needle with white yarn. Use a X stitch for the shamrocks, refer to diagram. When finished with the shamrocks, weave in yarn tails instead of using knots.

DIRECTIONS
Begin with GREEN yarn ch 34 loosely.

Foundation Row:
With GREEN yarn, 2nd ch sc, sc in each ch to the end, ch 1 turn.

ROW 1: With WHITE yarn, 2nd ch sc, sc in the back hook to the end, ch 1 turn.

ROW 2: With GREEN yarn, 2nd ch sc, sc to the end, ch 1 turn.

ROW 3: With GREEN yarn, 2sc in the 2nd ch, sc across last ch 2 sc, ch 1 turn.

ROW 4: With GREEN yarn, 2 sc in the 2nd sch, sc across, last ch 2 sc, ch 1 turn.

ROW 5 - 15: Repeat row 4.

ROW 16: With GREEN yarn, 1 sc in the 2nd ch, sc across, ch 1 turn.

ROW 17 -19: Repeat row 16.

ROW 20: Center of Shamrock afghan stitch and sl st on.

ROW 21-28: Repeat row 16, sl st around the afghan stitch.

ROW 29: With GREEN yarn sc in the 2nd ch, the next 5 ch sc, ch 1 turn.

ROW 30-35: Repeat Row 29.

ROW 29: Go back to row 29 skip 12 ch on 13 ch sc, in the next 38ch, ch 1 turn.

ROW 30: Skip 12 ch on 13 ch sc, in the next 38 ch, ch 1 turn.

ROW 31-15: Repeat row 30.

ROW 29: Go back to row 29, skip 12 ch on 13 ch sc, sc across to the end, ch 1 turn.

ROW 30: Skip 12 ch on 13 ch sc, sc across to the end, ch 1 turn.

ROW 31: Skip 12 ch on 13 ch sc, sc across to the end, ch 1 turn.

ROW 32-35: Repear row 31.

RIGHT LEG

Right Leg tie on with GREEN yarn sl st on row 29 ch 1, sc in each ch, sl st around, ch 12, and pick-up the side sl st around, and repeat 7 times.

LEFT LEG

Left Leg, tie on with GREEN yarn and repeat the same as right leg.

NECK BAND

ROW 36: Tie on GREEN yarn, in 3rd ch sc,m sc to the end, skip the 2 ch, sc in the last ch, ch 1 turn.

ROW 37-43: Repeat row 36.

ROW 44: With GREEN yarn, in 2nd ch sc to the end, ch 1 turn.

ROW 45: With WHITE yarn, in 2nd ch sc to the end, ch 1 turn.

ROW 46: With GREEN yarn, in 2nd ch, sc in the ch in the back hook, ch 1 turn.

FINISHING

With the sweater body put the right sides together start at Row 16 to Row 33 sl st together with GREEN yarn.

ENJOY THE DOG IN THE OUTFIT!!!

4ᵀᴴ OF JULY SWEATER

4th OF JULY SWEATER

Make Those Special Moments Even More Memorable With This American Tradition, The 4th Of July Sweater On Your Loveable Dog.

4TH Of JULY SWEATER

FINISHED SIZE
Approximately length small 20 x 21

Note: Length is measured from the base of neck of the dog to base of the dogs tall.

MATERIALS
2 Navy Lion Brand Yarn Wool-Ease Worsted Weight
1 White Lion Brand Yarn Wool-Ease Worsted Weight
1 Red Lion Brand Yarn Wool-Ease Worsted Weight

Size E

ADDREVIATIONS
dc		double crochet
sc		single crochet
ch		chain (s)
sl st		slip stitch
dec		decrease (s)
hdc		half double crochert
tr		treble crochet

4TH OF JULY SWEATER STARS

MAKE 7 With E Crochet Hook in WHITE Yarn

ROW 1: With WHITE yarn ch 5, join with sl st in first ch to form a ring.

ROW 2: Ch 2, work 14 hdc in ring, with sl st in top of ch 2.

ROW 3: *Ch 7, turn cl st in 2nd ch from hook, 1 sc in next ch, 1 hd in next ch, 1 dc in each
DIRECTIONS:
Of next 2 ch, 1 tr in next ch, skip 2 hdc of round 1, sl st in next hdc: repeat

From *4 times. Fasten off.

Begin ch 27 loosely with NAVY yarn, about 7" long,
Foundation Row:
With NAVY yarn, 3rd ch dc, dc in each ct to end, ch 2 turn.

ROW 1: With RED yarn, 3rd ch dc in the back hook to the end ch 2 turn.

ROW 2: With NAVY yarn, 3rd ch dc to the ned, ch 2 turn.

ROW 3: With NAVY yarn, 2 sc in the 2nd ch, sc across, last ch 2 sc ch 1 turn.

ROW 4: 2 sc in the 2nd ch, sc across, last ch 2 sc, ch 1 turn.

ROW 5: 2 sc in the 2nd ch, sc across, last ch 2 sc, ch 1 turn.

ROW 6: 2 sc in the 2nd ch, sc across, last ch 2 sc, ch 1 turn.

ROW 7: 2 sc in the 2nd ch, sc across, last ch 2 sc, ch 1 turn

ROW 8 - 15: Repeat Row 7.

ROW 16: With NAVY yarn, 1 sc in the 2nd ch, sc across, ch 1 turn.

ROW 17 - 28: Repeat Row 16.

ROW 29: With NAVY yarn sc in the 2nd ch, the next 5 ch sc, ch 1 turn.

ROW 30 - 35: Repeat Row 29.

ROW 29: Go back to row 29, with NAVY yarn skip 12 ch on 13 ch sc, in the next 38 ch, ch 1 turn.

ROW 30: With NAVY yarn skip 12ch on 13 ch sc, in the next 38 ch, ch 1 turn.

ROW 31 - 35: Repeat row 30.

ROW 29: With NAVY yarn skip 12 ch on 13 ch sc, sc across to the end, ch 1 turn.

ROW 30: With NAVY yarn skip 12 ch on 13 ch sc, sc across to the end, ch 1 turn.

ROW 31: With NAVY yarn skip 12 ch on 13 ch sc, sc across to the end, ch 1 turn.

ROW 32 - 35: Repeat row 31.

RIGHT LEG;

Tie on with NAVY yarn sl st on row 29 ch 1, sc in each ch, sl st around, ch 12, and pick-up the side sl st around, and repeat 7 times.

LEFT LEG,

Tie on with NAVY yarn and repeat the same as right leg.

NECK BAND

ROW 36: Tie on NAVY yarn, in 3rd ch sc, sc to the end, skip the 2ch, sc in the last ch, ch 1 turn.

ROW 37 - 43: Repeat row 36.

ROW 44: With NAVY yarn in 2nd ch sc to the end, ch 2 turn.

ROW 45: With RED yarn, in 3rd ch dc, dc in the ch, ch 2 turn.

ROW 46: With NAVY yarn in 3rd ch dc, dc in the ch in the back hook, ch 2 end.

Sew on the WHITE stars on the body with WHITE yarn, 2 stars at the bottom, 3 stars in the middle, and 2 stars on the top.

FINISHING

With the sweater body put the right sides together start at Row 16 to Row 33 sl st together with NAVY yarn.

ENJOY

SNOWMAN CHRISTMAS DOG SWEATER

SNOWMAN CHRISTMAS DOG SWEATER

Here's a dog sweater designed especially for the family pet to wear at the holiday season.

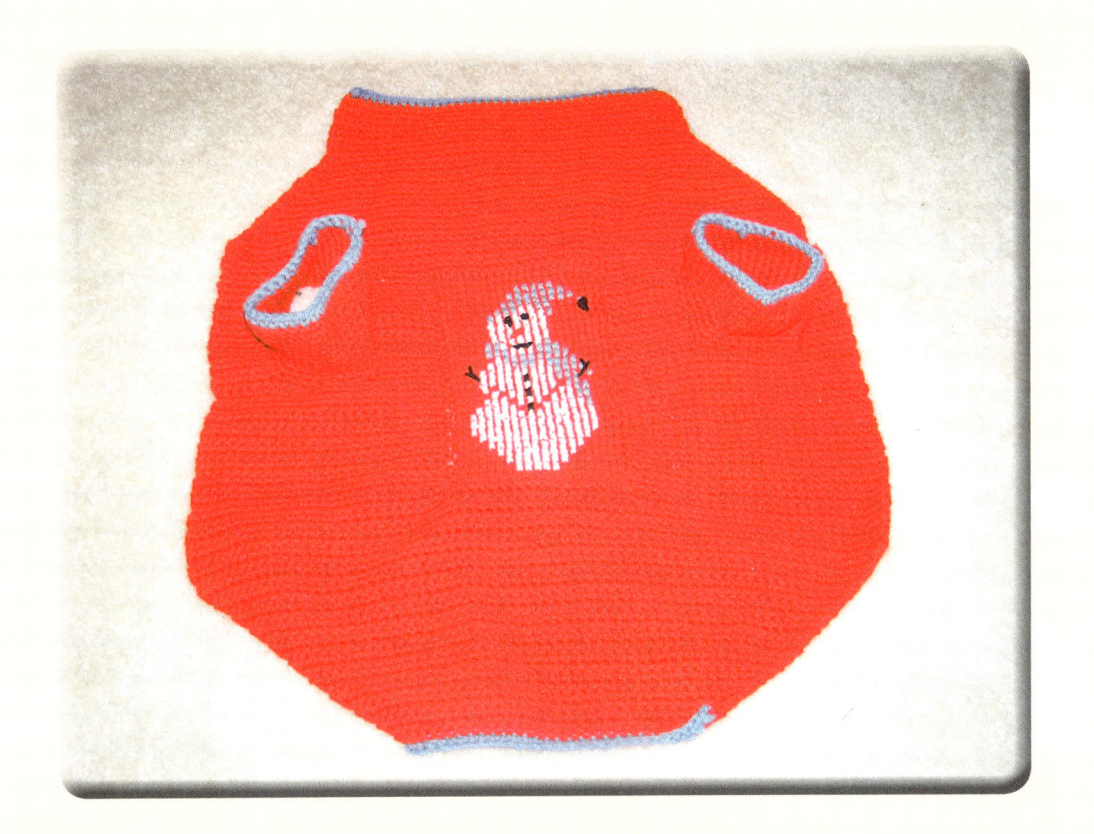

FINISHED SIZE
Approximately length small 20 x 21

Note: Length is measured from the base of neck of the dog to base of the dogs tail.

MATERIALS
2 Red Yarn
1 Light Blue Yarn
1 White Yarn
1 Black Yarn

Size G Crochet Hook

ADDREVIATIONS
ch	chains (s)
yo	yarn over
sc	single crochet
lp	loop (s)
sl st	slip stitch

SNOWMAN CHRISTMAS DOG SWEATER

AFGHAN STITCH FOR THE SNOWMAN

DIRECTIONS

With RED yarn ch 21 loosely.

ROW 1 Step 1: Keeping all lps on hook, pull up alp through top lp only, in 2nd ch from hook and each ch across - same number of lps and ch. Do not turn.

STEP 2: Yo and pull through first lp on hook, "yo and pull through 2 lps on hook, rep from * across (1 lp rem on hook for first lp of next row). Do not turn.

ROW 2: Step 1: Keeping all lps on hook, pull up a lp from under 2nd vertical bar, * pull up a lp from under next vertical bar, rep from * across. Do not turn.

STEP 2: Rep Step 2 of Row 1. Rep both steps of Row 2 for required for 11 Rows. Fasten off after last row by working a sl st in each bar across. When the 11 Rows are finished, it is a perfect grid for cross-stitch for the 3 white shamrocks.

EMBROIDERY STITCHES
To embellish a crocheted piece with embroidery, thread a large-eyed yarn needle with White Yarn. Use a X stitch for the snowman, refer to diagram. When finished with the snowman, weave in yarn tails instead of using knots.

Snowman

X in WHITE
O in BLACK
Z in BLUE

DIRECTIONS
Begin with blue yarn ch 31 loosely.

FOUNDATION ROW:
With BLUE yarn, 2nd ch sc, sc in each ch to the end, ch 1 turn.

ROW 1: With BLUE yarn, 2nd ch sc, sc in the back hook to the end, ch 1 turn.

ROW 2: With RED yarn, 2nd ch sc, sc to the end, ch 1 turn.

ROW 3: With RED yarn, 2sc in the 2nd ch, sc across, last ch 2 sc, ch 1 turn.

ROW 4: With RED yarn, 2 sc in the 2nd ch, sc across, last ch 2 sc, ch 1 turn.

ROW 5 - 15: Repeat row 4.

ROW 16: With RED yarn, 1 sc in the 2nd ch, sc across, ch 1 turn.

ROW 17: Repeat row 16.

ROW 20 - 27: Repeat row 16.

ROW 28: Center the Snowman afghan stitch and sl st on.

ROW 29: With RED yarn sc in the 2nd ch, the next 5 ch sc, ch 1 turn.
ROW 30-35: Repeat Row 29.

ROW 29: Go back to row 29 skip 12 ch on 13ch sc, in the next 38 ch, ch 1 turn.

ROW 30: Skip 12 ch on 13 ch sc, in the next 38 ch, ch 1 turn.

ROW 31 - 35: Repeat row 30.

ROW 29: Go back to row 29, ship 12 ch on 13 ch sc, sc across to the end, ch 1 turn.

ROW 30: skip 12 ch on 13 ch sc, sc across to the end, ch 1 turn.

ROW 31: Skip 12 ch on 13 ch sc, sc across to the end, ch 1
Turn.

ROW 32 - 35: Repeat row 31.

RIGHT LEG
Tie on the RED yarn sl st on row 29 ch 1, sc in each ch, sl st around, ch 12, and pick-up the side sl st around, and repeat 6 times. The last row sc in BLUE yarn.

LEFT LEG
Tie on with RED yarn and repeat the same as right leg.

NECK BAND
ROW 36: Tie on RED yarn, in 3rd ch sc, sc to the end, skip the 2 ch, sc in the last ch, ch 1 turn.

ROW 37 - 43: Repeat row 36.

ROW 44: With RED yarn in 2nd ch sc in the end, ch 1 turn.

ROW 45: With RED yarn, in 2nd ch sc to the end, ch 1 turn.

ROW 46: With BLUE yarn in 2nd ch, sc in the ch in the back hook, ch 1 turn.

FINISHING

With the sweater body put the right sides together start at Row 16 to Row 33 sl st together with RED yarn.

ENJOY!

AUTHOR

Linda has a degree in Culinary Arts and is a practicing Massage Therapist and Esthetician. In addition, she enjoys traveling and arts and crafts. This picture was taken in Alaska while her and her husband, Larry, were enjoying playing with Alaskan Huskies at a musher's camp.

CPSIA information can be obtained at www.ICGtesting.com
Printed in the USA
BVIW12n2055020118
503998BV00011B/119